EDGE OF FIRE

TIM BRIGHT

Copyright © 2024 Tim Bright
All rights reserved
First Edition

PAGE PUBLISHING
Conneaut Lake, PA

First originally published by Page Publishing 2024

ISBN 979-8-89315-909-7 (pbk)
ISBN 979-8-89315-925-7 (digital)

Printed in the United States of America

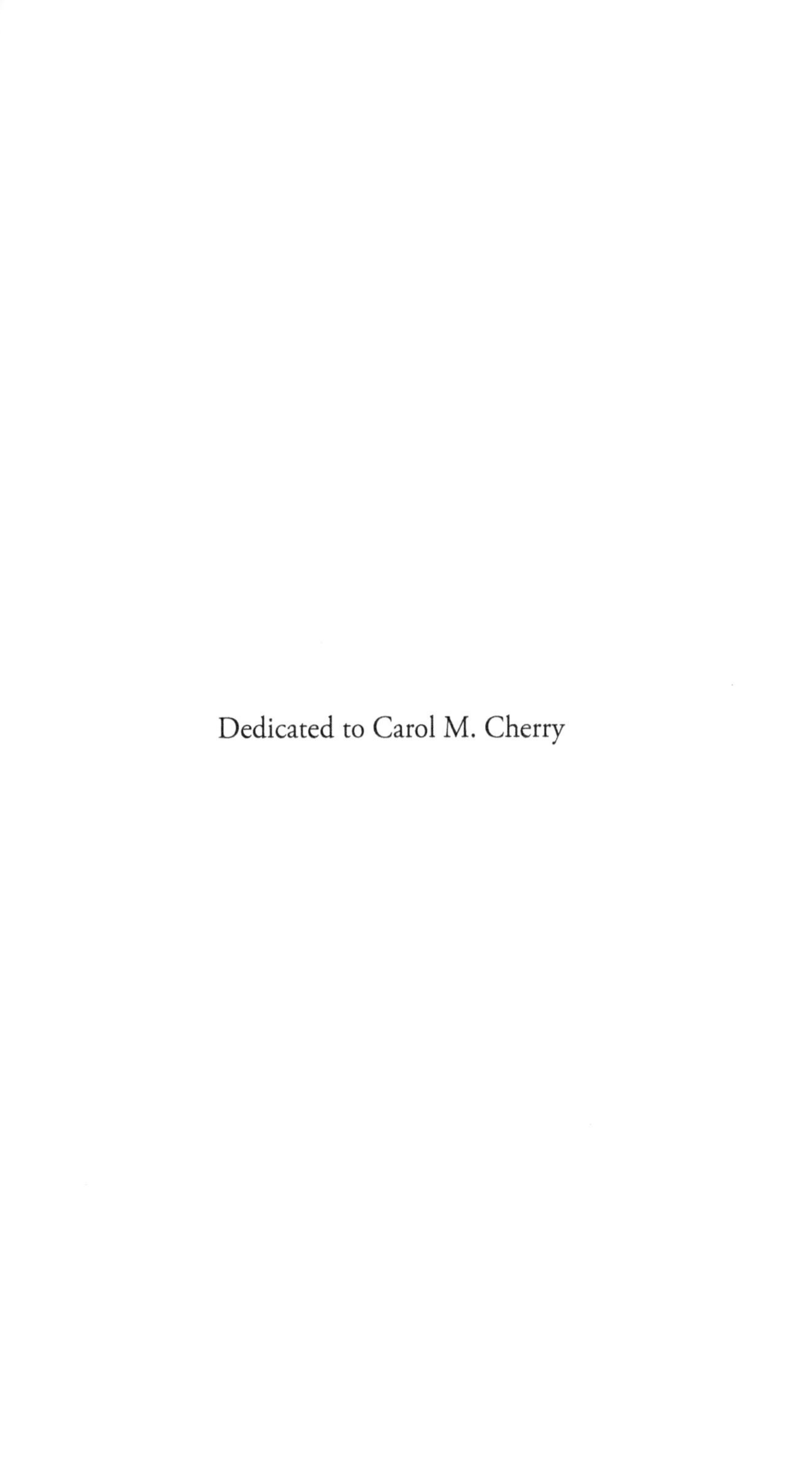

Dedicated to Carol M. Cherry

The Door

Through the blackened
door.

It is another time and
place. He walks on sandy soil
without sense of being.

A black window carved by night.
White muntins take their place
and give the choir their cue
to begin the song of love.

It is a blue sky today, unblemished
by winter's grind. At the horizon,
it sinks to dark.

The pines have grown
to powerful heights, to pace the sun
of blistering heat and light.

Through the blackened door, it's indeed
a different time and place.
Mood has changed. Feelings
are in play. Truth has taken
a useless seat, and to many, okay.

Toy

Thin line as a
forest with a side.

I grip my lip, soft, pliable
sinking slowly. It's
a beginning to an end.

The end is dark, like a fountain
pen seated
on a red table.

Somewhere in the last
chapter, I remember that
tree bent out of shape, part
of a memory growing smaller.

Tomb

Slanting floor,
a window.

Then the black
pastor, her knees hidden
behind strands.

The environment
is caustic with needles.

In Night's Cover

In night's cover,
a strong, persistent
fever that will not let
up despite the will.

Nothing is pure as if
this time is made for it.

The ugly thrive on
uncertainty and make
fools of the wise.

We struggle to live the
right way, but denied time
and again.

I have lived the span.
What's the answer?

Who Is Alone

I do not breath,
but the breath of loneliness.

Loneliness has currency.
Attracts the famished
crowd.

It's a state of being. You can't forget.
Live it.

There is a door in the
sky. It is flapping on hinges
on a storm cloud.

Restricted

Restricted colors, deep
yellows, morning.

It splashes a pocket of silver
against a wizened tree.

In the cold, the
silver expands, jumping
across to other trees, touching tiny
branches on the way. Paintings in a cover
of gray wait in repose
for me to turn.

I am lost in thought. I see the ends
that give. I am tight and hidden.

Future

In bone of life I
live. In bone of death
my future lies. There is
no dispute where I am.
Do I tread on old floors
and eye old photographs
of those I loved, a fragment of
what I know in this emerging world?
Not conscious, but it's the next
step I take. Be careful.
Watch the world. Watch where the cat
runs. I feel strength of a tall pine.

Ordinary Life

Odd to be left here without
the usual formula, the usual
type of fallback. We are the type
that when he comes in the
door, we respond or do not, thinking
it's happened before, this day
on the porch, this afternoon.

We think we're the same, like
our neighbor cutting his grass,
watching a bird find old grass for
a nest.

Even if your neighbor is walking
the road and you stop to say hello,
don't be upset if he doesn't want
to talk. It's his type when you, for
some reason, don't fit. The world
turns like this: energy is released,
and you and he go separate ways.

Distant House

Distant line of power,
lateral shift to make its
form. Morning's aggressive sun
assumes control of forest.
It blasts the shackles
from sluggish night,
scraping bits and pieces.

A reflection digs into
black entanglements
to gaze at the yellow show.

Black animals roam, slump
their backs against prickly
orange. Dark threads of ivy
penetrate nooks. Make
the forest ancient,
dark.

Panes of Glass

Night panes, a deeper
thought. Panes of glass,
colony of thought—to find a way out of
hurt. They too are houses with
strange and awkward structures,
filled with water sluicing out
privileged land. The land is
barren. Nothing to be seen, yet
we go there.

In sharp light of a pane, we bond.
Step out of it. We are human, clothed
in ordinariness. We look for fun.
We love sex. We seek the ordinary all
around us. When is next,
car trip?

Balloon

We
see it as a star, unblemished
in its frame, going up
into blue, now light.
It cuts the hill; we see it
go, now distant and a blur.
What did it mean when
it was here, so full and
robust, wearing its stripes
for cities and towns to admire?
Instantly, a silhouette.

Meeting a Neighbor

I could have met him on
a plane, the cool heat
of the unknowable.

You're in the stratosphere,
zooming. Friendly tones are
admissible.

I might like you, feeling or it's
business. I had questions about
Ephesians and Paul.
We moved on.

The Bible is a bore, was the impression,
though he was a retired minister.
He wanted the nitty-gritty, how
I was ticking.

I didn't tick right. A big downdraft.
However, he liked my
three parakeets.

When he visited, he would
stare at them.

Finally, he told me to pack it in.
I said no way.

Black as Pitch

A shadeless tree, black
in the morning against white
to its feet. A soul-cutting corners
on edges of a universe hidden
from telescopes. Our very souls
probe its being without a penny's
worth of truth except to lock our eyes
on what's more to see. Fare thee well, tree,
in your venture of a lifetime
to probe the indifferent clouds,
to see if anyone has the courage
to climb.

One Shot

One shot into darkness.
Who thought it would be this?
Despite the catcalls, we ran
up a tree. Nothing to see
there, but my mother said,
"Here we are." It's time.

I have heard that before.
It didn't make much difference.
Opposites attract. but it
can be death. The grave is
not far. A better course.
If it's not pretty when it's done,
who will know?

The stench. Being alone is
part of the game.
But that word says
too much. It flows
without a punch.

But it's done, no retreat.
Laugh it off.

By the Shore

when I saw her swimming
in the bay, into angles
of waves, into angles of
surf.

When a clock is wound and
I appear out of death, out
of a closet in new clothes.

I saw her in the waves,
the fomenting waves rising
to the shore.

I didn't say goodbye to
her. It was too late; the sun
was blazing on me, making me
pure.

No more this fragile man.

Land

We think much about
the land we live on.
It has small trees generally.
Sand dunes are bright
with sun.

But on this day
everything is glum, stuck-on
chewing gum. Half my window
is badges of black,
half below the earth
near Hell with
beeps of muted fire.

Lessons of life
come in different ways. They
issue through holes in an
avalanche.

What's the point of killing
thousands of people to prop
your ego?

Black Rock

There's a black rock in the
niche of a tree. Without
stands the tree; its hollow
is plain to see.
Afternoon sun and
clouds give it distinction.

I don't know what to
make of it. Why nature
intervened to give it
dominance.

The answer came when
I took another look and
noticed a turkey settling
into the niche as nightfall
came.

Long Way

At the edge of the line
It doesn't make sense.

Now the line is tapering,
requiring swift action.
Now it seems a picture of
the times. One photo of many
lost.

It's a haven for those who
seep into power and want
to languish there for good. Kudos
to the selfless brave who see
the mentals shining and want to close
out their unearned check forever.

These Days

It is regular to barf
in the deep silence of a day;
to find a hideout without
regret—let go of the vital
spirit hanging carelessly.

Goodwill is becoming scarce
in the tumult of illogic.

We are pawns on a chessboard
cracking.

Game

The game of
distraction with trees popping
up, hair falling over eyeglasses,
thoughts of past friends, current
friends, hair in my eyes.

Will John check on the snowblower
before winter? Will I see the enemy
in darkness? These are things that
haunt me like hunting for something
I will never find. I might see it
in a haze, at a distance, on a star at night,
blinking.

The same with chess,
although I'm not to be outdone.

You visualize a good move
coming up in the endgame.
The endgame is sparse, with many
vacant squares. One way or another,
pieces disappear, and I'm
counting my chances.

Turkeys

In feathered black,
jaunty steps across the abyss,
they shift. No care for oblique
world except the macadam.

Dimensionless are they, drum beats
away from the intolerable world
they occupy, bearing nothing
but long black feathers,
stringy legs, sharp
eyes.

Their care for the day
is forever, more grass to
forage in.

Belly Fight

Although tired of
war, he and his men moved
east. In rags of coats and shirts,
they pushed on into dirt and
layers of leaves, colors of rust
and brown; many blackened
with age. Water they needed.
It came cold or frozen.

From afar, scouts waved them
on. Hit by blasts of wind, they
bent to keep men safe. Through
compounded earth, they escaped to
see the other side: an ocean.

Stairway

I drink my coffee
slick and dry,
a knife to
wake the mind clogged
with whatever.

Not healthy. It reeks of
whatever, a song caught
in overdrive and smelling
of scraping threads. It's not cool.
There's so much
rubbish to throw away.
I can hear it on streets, prancing
on pins.

The smell of the mind.
It reconnoiters to begin the day,
a pile you can sense five miles away.

What happened on this silky
morning? No one knows except forest
slumbering over the sky.

I am left without a drink of water.
A shower will be in the past.
Coyote slinks away.

Pearly Voice

To talk to a pearly
voice is enchanting.
It flows in valleys of
regret. The flow is incessant,
as if no end to the dream.

Shadows of trees sing
to a canoe striking against
the current.

The pearly voice strangles
me to a life all its own.

In Glory Might I Live

Cars speed by on the
way to oblivion. Gray stalks of
trees do not faze them,
though part of the scenery.
Cars bubble and heave on the
way to a summer destination.

Summer is real, and they glorify
themselves; they have made
a home in someone else's home.

So they claim a cigarette or pot
for vacant mouths with jibber
on the lower lip.

Trees buckle and sway,
pretending they are
lost to what is going on.

They are rooted to the earth
but need relief from the hurly-burly
of man's disturbance.

The sweetness of grass is becoming
apparent, singing to the stillness
of afternoon.

The Veil

Easy to see the
faults. Not so easy to forget,
with a flick of the mind,
what you have built over
the years.

Then a break, a fissure
in the wall. You backdrop.
Think twice about
this granular state of being,
wishing for a glorious day,
not the frantic passing
of time. We live it unabashed,
with consequences, multiplying
dread and a need to
escape to a foreign city or village,
to see you.

It Is Not Doable

It is not doable to live
this way with buckle bones
and balance awry.

So it is with a vein-winged fly
who tries to break the pane
of glass to escape my prison.

Fragment

Through the gloom of
a window pane half
submerged in a haze of whiteness,
I imagine a circus
of scenes connecting to
pillars of Rome. Pine trees
stand tall, resolute, withstanding
ugliness of hurricanes, heavy
desolate rain, insufferable heat of
summer on pine needles,
the cold of winter.

It's a march into memory.

Bicycles carry light of the sun
to territory never seen.
Children bring circus to
the street. A bird jams the
light, his eyes keen on
a soft melody of green.

Beach of Trash

On a beach of trash
we throw our
lips with glee. There they
rot in front of wilting palaces.

With slow regret, I
notice the cancellation
and wonder what is next.

Dark Passage

Clouds beckon but none
respond. The earth prefers
a stand, no matter.
The haunted one-light
house shivers in the
storm. The inhabitants lie
on floors not to be seen.
Fences they build but then take
them down. But grass
grows despite it all as a
squirrel manages the farm;
keeps peace among the neighbors
with journeys to and fro and
up bewildering heights of the
pines.

The scab of darkness remains
as we retreat to silos of content
to rummage in solitary thought.
I'm no longer needful to join
a group that might turn the plate
upside down. Thinking now, it's
necessary to protect my soul.

In the back, silence is
profound. It grows even more
with the loss of scampering
chipmunks living happily under
the shed.

Oblivion

To die on a line
of a bough and
never see the end.

It is frightening to
be there without a friend or
foe. So what matters
in this carved-out world
is peace, a sense of
happiness that does not
leave you in the lurch.

To bend in the lurch
and feel the break,
the crack, the inevitable
slide to oblivion.

Faces

Faces in the tree
that mix in this troubled
time with others not
willing to show true intent.
I could not name them.
They disappear then appear
in another time. Obscurity
is the theme as all dance
to an equal beat. Dance with
the same emotion as death would not
let it. Rusty fields beneath
reckless living are not
exhibiting emotion. Content they
are to lay flat, to admire
the rain, curl in the hot sun.
But in this convolution of boughs,
faces grow thin, remnants of
old men and women. They taper
to a pyramid to disappear

Mighty Pines

It is difficult to imagine a
tall pine tree as still.
On a passive day, it might
appear still, but on another, it
might be on the verge of
thrashing my house.

It is an awkward structure
except for the trunk, which
rams straight into mist
and clouds.

Boughs have a haphazard
way of expressing themselves.
They do not give a hoot
which way they go. The mission
is not direction but action
no matter. Probability
is more the right term than
scientific prediction. The
massing of needles, which
blank out the sky, create misgivings,
angry faces.

We Live

When the slow and
craving mix with delight,
the heat of a stove
burner lives a life
not imagined.

The freak shadow of
a pine bough is
eclipsed by stars of
life.

This crummy song
is too loud.

The Plain Old Plain

The daily drag hits me
hard as if a target for the
disturbed. The stubborn lines
of the window try to keep
me on track. I'm in a
seat of an empty baseball
park with lights shut off after a
night game. With the roofs of
surrounding buildings fading
away.

The window lock
is in place as it has been all
winter. What to say before
lunch of peanut butter and blueberry
jam on one slice of hearty white
bread. What to say in a tranquil
moment with nature moving my
way. My body accepts the verdict
with a sag in the seat.

From peak to peak, a great
swath of granular gray. A belly
of gray dumps gray into
a belly ripped on one side.
Belly days large and small.
Boughs stuck together,
stuck to white for the day and night.

But it doesn't change
politicians from ripping their
noses off to say something
important.

Yet, I keep saying to myself,
I am alive, at least for now.

On the Sandbars

Waves retreat with
a line of sea beyond a
stretch of sand.

A man sits alone in a hollow
of sand. His hair tousled with
bits of sand. He seems like
still wind, no object, no
frustration, only sitting carelessly
waiting for a dream.

But, yet, there is action in the
body as though it waits for
him to think of an act.
But it only lasts, retreats into
a languid pose, his eyes searching
the outline of the town.

His wife, not far away,
smiles at whatever she
smiles at—a ghost calls it.
It is a ghost, she thinks, when
it appears in a white sheet.
The boulders of the breakwater seem
warm to her as brilliant sunlight
splashes them. But too tired
to go see. Is there something I need,
she thinks, gripping dry white sand.

Bough

At a weathered bough he
thought of the remains of
his life, now an image of
what it was. A fragment in
the grind to make it
meaningful.

In the rain, was it his fault—
the many woes? The visions
of what he was and might be
crossed and repeated the danger
of disownment. He hung to the
piece that made him a player
in a flexing, disturbing scene.

Slowly the work progressed
as though a map of the past
being drawn. He was a player,
perhaps a bit player.

Vacuums are strong.
It's not important what is
or what was—"There you are,"
she said. And background,
at moments, is everything
before it disappears.

I pick up the leaves.
Sort their colors.

Computer Repair Woman

Above the roof
I hear her yelling,
a dull scream as if
a high-speed car wreck
in progress.

It is a guttural scream
at birth. But it comes out
of a wreck—a mechanical
spin that scratches
the soul.

Into Night

Into darkness
he prowled for warmth
and people.
Like a scarecrow out of
place, he wandered, never
thinking he might be a
jerk.

On he moved to find a seat at
the bar. People crunched their
heads to view this specimen
of humanity. He viewed
them back wondering at
the interest. Wasn't he one them,
he thought. So let's get along.

Out of weirdness
of balls of lights, he sniffed
the white shirt of the bartender.
The skin of his face made a strong
impression. He ordered a grasshopper
from a thought he had years ago.

It was green-colored.

The alcohol tingled in his throat.
But he felt contact with the
people was sharp. He sidled off
barstool, headed to the
door.

Out on a slimy gray
Sidewalk, he walked, no longer
thinking.

Inch by Inch

As spring begins
I sit quietly at its progress.
It's not be outdone by March,
a curmudgeon in many houses.
Spring oozes along, a trickle
of ancient times, demonstrating
its vigor and need to hold its own.

The season break is upon us.
Time to remember,
not move it into memory's over
loaded vault.

Like an anchored barge
March holds on with cold
fists, withstanding the silent
blows that say move on.

A Circle

I drew a circle
around a running man.
He ran fast into a forest.

It was a lake he
cherished. A place
he wanted to die.

In the dissected world
he ran not afraid of
bears or mountain lions
that prowled the inch.

He embraced the lake. Took
a swim. Saw trout,
small-mouthed bass, pickerel
swimming into a
path sinking to darkness.

He felt coolness.

Forever the fish.
Forever the lake.

Mystery

The forms by dark and
light then the
evolution of a building then
a couple in an awkward
relation. Is what seems natural
actually an absurdity?

I did not know at the moment
what to draw other than a
contradiction. It wasn't true—
this structure I was led to
believe. A melting of truth.
A beginning of discovery.

Flower

The bleached white seems
out of place in this frame
of rough weather.

The hollow of light from
above, perhaps not unusual
to the artist. This drear of light
munches on the fabric of air.

Bright yellow petals
split defining their
birth.

An eruption occurs, sends
petals in every direction.
Strangely, they cling stubbornly
to its spine.

A peripatetic vase with
gauzy lips puckers at the
thought of this magnificent flower
holding the key to rapturous
love.

Calls Him a Name

In idleness she talks as
if on cue. It seems that
idle is the seamless way to go.
As when my brother and she took
a walk with me among the hills
of Ireland, she gave me
the stare of disapproval.
Or when she waits in the front
seat to retort something I have said.
Or at a party, I tried to soften
the threads of dislike; her voice
turned to active mode to shove me
into the closet of numbness.
Or on the eve of leaving Ireland,
she leaned from the car to say goodbye
but instead said, "You are a coward."

Haze

In a weakening sky
pine needles shrink to
clumps. I watch the
scene unfold; a serious drama
of morning's overture.

Boughs with heavy loads
expand into shapeless forms,
senseless in their expression.

The hopeless point of
the tree, leached of its energy
by the laziness of the air.

But
the pine leans into a
vacuum, lifts its load,
waits for a change.

Density of the Forest

On the slightest thought
I move to what little I
have to say.
It seems as thin
as hair. Into deeper thought I
try.

The mind, asleep,
wakes to the splendor of
morning. Takes care of the
forest leaves; touches them
through the pane of glass.

While upward I gaze at a
lonely sky, its transparent blue
runs to the horizon.

Into the forest go my
eyes searching for the
slightest to catch my attention.

It is here I live in spirit and
thought. Rudiments of
civil living begin here, although
forgotten.
Our universe is here—
not there.

Morning Blues

Languid, disruptive.
If I think this way,
nothing will happen.
The sun will disappear,
then patches of
black on grass. A robin won't
stop on the head of statue.

The beginning of
spring. I see my blankets
on the bed in turmoil, red and
black—twisting. They have a
penchant for it.

Morning sun pickles a
tall pine as white turns
ugly in a mixture of
black.

Macadam shatters under
relentless rays of sun.
Begins to bubble.

Night

In the vast night
threads are tiny.

Nothing to comprehend
in the shining.

The wondering hopeless in
a meek world without content.

We live on sharp edges
with only an abysmal cry.

There should be more to say,
but time is short.

O Find That Life

O find that life in
murky swell and by the
murderer's heap we will.
Buy the sword, wipe the
blood. It will be needed
in a week.

The light, the blink of lights,
the rancid pile,
to clean up the neighborhood.
We will cut off what is left of him.
We stagger with work to build
our fences to practice in
private with our AR-15.

The murky structure is deep, sinks even
farther, but cares run otherwise.
To pray, to say the mantra, never again.
Make sure AR-15 is ready
at the hip. Black is black, but only if we
say so, and only then.

Afternoon

Haze drifts ever slowly
into pine boughs, breaking
them apart, disintegrating the
thinnest. An irregular shape of
red anticipates a maroon, then
slices fading purple.

Wind tears at the top,
pushes havoc into a harvest
of black boughs.

Next day,
cliff of swimming fish.
Dangling in the distance,
a hanged man flutters his
hands in panic.

I am calm. My eyelids barely
move. I watch a cactus grow.
A clam on sand burrows for safety.

Dead calm at the beach.
No seagulls fluttering to make
a landing. No people
walking. A lighthouse
stares down oblivion.

Dry air tortures death.
I hear a vacant call of
a grotesque shadow.

Guillotine

In the court of death,
guillotine is best.

When One Half

When one-half becomes
important, you lose track
of thought. You're not alone.

You live on the golden river
far beyond the whitest clouds.
You rub shoulders with the
infinite and Papa Joe's Diner.

You eat cactus. You drink
drops of water. You realize
no end to time.

Imagination trembles. Your
skull has many curves in
the eye socket.

Afternoon turns to ghosts.

Grim

In the dirty areas, they
exist as if they were made
for it. Scavenging for trouble
to screw it into victory
is the ultimate. In the
innocence of the land,
they perpetuate the death
of thousands, soiling
sheets to cover it. They are content
in their haunts of death to sully
the fabric of everything.

O May

O grim May, far
away from what I
thought you would be.
The edge of a blunted
sword that cuts either way.

I want it to be a happier
time for nature, who chews
on earth with floods, hurricanes,
and tornadoes.

Will it not forgive the
wanton damage perpetrated
on it?

Are we not a greedy
lot who savors the flesh
and bone of all?
That flies and crawls
on earth with guns
and knives and clever
machines to strip what
is before it?

A Long Slog

You have to batten
down living
among the trees.

They might resent you,
or call you out for
making too much noise.

In their peaceful abode—
number 1 is keeping
quiet.

I heard trees will be cut
down, a forest of trees,
so bullets can fly, and walls
for protection. If unwanted
people show up, a barrage of
bullets will greet them.

So much for the identity
of a tree.

Girls Before Women

Girls before women is often
mistaken.
Women then girls.

It fits nicely into a society
hell-bent on making girls—women,
women—girls, girls—girls, and
women—women. Whichever rings
the cash register is society's way of
thinking. As a thinker remarked:
"America's business is business,"
opens the door to everything.
Good souls are picking
plastic off the beaches of Easter
Island, once a bastion of cultural
interest, now a dump for
everything.

Paintings of
melting clocks says it all.

Blame

I am further down than
before, yet he blames
me.

He has me in a hole
but left without a goodbye.

He thought my car key
was his, but when I wanted
it back, his face turned gray.
He puffed his way
out the door, made sounds
between his teeth.

He walks the street with
a limp, shakes a foot a little.

Two letters in vain to mend
our ways, but I came
to realize the knife is in.

Inflammatory

When skyscrapers are painted
red and fingernails
zebra stripes, will that be the
end of the act? "Many more," he
said, jerking his lips.

I am not here to clamor
but to impress—to make loud
noises and see fireworks light
the night. We are here to grin,
to grimace; to eat a hamburger
in between.

What else? The hamburger
man said when his stand fell apart
among thieves eating more.
A bullet he took with tumult all
around.

Such was his anguish,
with a school principal gasping in
his pocket, fat buses
pulverizing bicycles in their paths.

Ho-ho-ha-ha—the passengers sang
their blank stares of the day.

Bring Myself

To bring myself for
a beginning. How many
times must I start? The
background littered with
them. How many duplications
are there? Many cobwebs
on the way?

Characters you have to avoid.
Smells of sweetness you come across.
Empty men becoming the rule.
Watch the coming light.
Changing colors, fading grays.

A picture emerging. We are not
the same. A change is
required in the
hell.

Go on: this mush is an
embarrassment.

Colorful

In the back there
is this machine that
fills every hole and dent.

It's automatic. By it
flows a haze that paints
the color of a solemn
sky.

The street is flatter than
it is, while trees of all
sorts sink into a bland
soup.

Automatic is key,
bringing life to its
knees, ordering life
as if a recipe.

This day is not necessary.
Broadway's forms are true
but of another time.

The abstraction on my lawn
struggles, but it
too is smothered
in sameness.

Distance

Clouds are long, in your face,
this ripped-down
day.

A gaping
mouth of a crocodile.

I push away the stench of
life to seek a way. It
sucks—this constant pull
to oblivion.

Farther away would be relief.
Living on the edges of a
mountain is right.

I leave my thought to the wind,
their feelings unheard, their
mass of old. I shrink.

I'm a stranger in strange
local. Won't be heard again.
I shrink, a leaf of yore.

Didn't Know

I didn't know it
could be so still
like a museum of mummies.
Aren't we all?

A word from one is
the same from another.
So we find our comfort.

Nothing could be so bleak
to know we could stand for another
and count with ease
the blank of another.

So we go, stepping on
another without realizing
we step on ourselves.

Killing

Killing
innocent people who struggle
for existence, to live
honorably.

But who cares? Life goes on everywhere
Else—unabated, undeterred.

Some will be buried, others will
rot in the sun, in the rain.

Perpetrators live on, happy, vindicated—
a dream they have lived all their
lives.

Feast

In the feast of the
living, I do not dwell.
From outside, I hear the
crow call. His flapping wings
are praise to all protecting the land.

Aghast! There is no reform
except what is forced upon us.
We shake the land with
progress, behead the turkey for
our delight and unity, and make
soup of him as an afterthought.

Hooray to the man for the new tire,
the man for fitting ten more passengers
in a plane, lops off mountain tops to
dig more coal.

Is that True?

Love comes easy in
streets of paradise.
A mowing machine grinds
grass, spits it into
crocodile mouth. It's
at the entrance guarding its
young, waiting for grandma
to wander to the edge of
the lake. So turns savagery
to keep it going. How about
a nuclear plant?

Forms

Shapless forms mumble
in my kitchen, a primitive ritual.

In life—cabinets,
a shocking dark green you
see in a cave with bats
flying crazily.

In the wild
of this day, heaped with
clouds shines in
one spot, hides the sun.

Beyond the shine, a dreariness
coughs up more dreariness,
slides away behind
a church of pine trees.

The humor has
dissipated to a mournful
cry of vapidity.

Morning Glow

Such is this morning,
with stripes of blue, it
augurs well.

Suddenly, the forest grows cold
and black, as if an evil spirit
dwells. Have I leaped too
soon for contentment
when obvious danger
lurks?

Am I a false optimist
with cruelty on the rise? Wake,
wake, the village of fools and savages
is being built.

Where from Here

Pine needles
bunched together in a blanket,
threaded over many times.

Darkness
is the theme as you travel in
its midst. Not a whit of light.

A black mark on the sky,
not used to being upstaged.

Out from this horrific cloud comes
this branch, a lean black muscle.

A great fish soars in the
white, dipping here, bulging
its muscle up. I get it—
it is life, where it dips
and sways, rises
through the ether like a shark after
prey.

Night is closing with clumps of blackness
never seen.

Land of the Tree

In the land of the
tree, I feel the hardness.
I feel the endurance.
I feel the resilience that
has made you. There is
nothing that you have
not faced to be a tree.
I have not seen the recognition
you deserve except in
fleeting places. We do not
measure our growth in terms
of you, but in terms
of your destruction.

Winter Storm

A giraffe's neck
sweeps the coldness
of the air.

I feel it inside;
even two coats are not
enough. I watch the
snow blast.

I wonder, as winter draws
to a close, what's
next?

Climate change
not so fast.

There is more to
come. I will take what is
mine.

Poem Too

Sit by the sea,
its quiet waves that never leave.
I feel the flow
of it, like an uninterrupted
wave sweeping all before it.

I say to the sea, I'm here
and I want to stay right here
even if you want to wash me
away.

From afar, the sea gazes
at me as if it didn't understand;
as if I am a sandbar to wash
away.

The Morning Show

Fog is taking
its time disseminating to
the bay.

Coalescing into a droplet
of water, the white house
seems mournful, crouched in trees.

I sit wrapped
in a down vest, waiting for March
to give up its grudge and give
April a chance.

Patches of black on white
in a painting, we step
from one detail to another, measuring
in our imagination how they fit.

We step from rust of leaves to dark
hollows to a long dark passage
of a tree. It goes until a bit of cloud
intervenes.

Potomac

Is a river a cesspool?

With a luster of emerald
Green, your eyes will
encompass it from
over there to here. No matter how
it's figured: North-South, East-West,
the luster is there.

By chance, you take a sip
and survive, you will fit in
the marathon.

The neightboring trees are sinful.
Their vigor, no doubt, a joke
to Potomac's flow.

Push

Heated air pushes
deformed thoughts.

Deformity of thought catches
the crazies who see a stop sign
to think green. Their lives
a metaphor for how not live
but cogitate nevertheless. We
hold onto trees except when they
get in the way. Their bravery is
astounding in this cockroach
down-middle world.

They Meet

Eye to eye they meet,
their hands beside their pockets.
No expression of distress to meet the hurdles
of the day. Their fingers twitch
behind the scenes, they snicker
behind the teeth.

They count the money
on the roll, not afraid to over count.
He said it was a game, but they're not
afraid to say it's not.

Games for children.
But it's a different time.
It requires different thinking.

At the rally. He pointed to the graph
that said what he said. They wore different
hats. A different mode would bother them.

She Took Me Through

She took me through
the window of life and
gave me sustenance to the
grave.

Death is before me, beetle-eyed.
I wait for the ceiling to collapse.

It won't be a shadow that emerges
but a verdict. It will be waiting
in a wood cold and dank.

When the Blue?

When the blue arrives I'll give
it a thought. My thoughts
a whirl. Breakfast done.
Bowl empty—hard, dried
oatmeal along bowl's
edges. Testimony to stringent
living. Thought too is
stringent—sun-dried rocks
on a beach.

I live in that
corridor, but is becoming more
narrow. Good for a fly.

We are soaking with rain, way above
average for March. Going out with
a wet whimper. Window exposes
grim light over forest.

An enormous crab clawing
its way forward to claw my head.

Socket

My eyes droop
to the socket's bottom
to rest from work.

The brick-brack of pine needles;
faces appear
grimacing, smiling.

My eyes rise to point
out rolling masses of leaves
traveling to the coal factory.

I put a hand over my eyes
to see a merry-go-round
with flashing lights, workmen
in yellow suits, a bull is
running wild.

Wind

Branch goes into
incantations; sweeps
a lady's veil.

Pine needles spear the living
chitter-chatter by the wall.

This day announces a dreary past;
gives me pause to think, what's what?

Nothing so bold as a windy
branch carving meat out of the sky.
The smell is horrendous, drowns
the clear-eyed boy.

It plows ahead and wrecks
an oncoming fool. It knows we are
stalks in a screwy universe.

But forges ahead despite its rakish
past.

About the Author

Tim Bright graduated from the University of Virginia with a bachelor's degree. He began his career as a fine artist, studying with Edwin Dickinson at the Art Students League in New York City and Karl Knaths in Provincetown. Several years later, he became a builder, constructing several houses, including his own. When he retired from the business, he moved to Ireland for a short time. While there he developed an interest in poetry. He has been writing for the past ten years. At one time, he led a writing group at the Wellfleet Writer's Guild. He studied with Rosalind Pace and Tony Hoagland. He has written five books: *Aftermath, Reflections, Sky Lion, Reality Between Events,* and *The Edge of Fire.*

www.ingramcontent.com/pod-product-compliance
Lightning Source LLC
Chambersburg PA
CBHW022051150726
47990CB00003B/1042